whatmusicmeanstome.org
rrejinophotography@me.com

Design by Richard Rejino

Cover, *Caroline*, 2009

Printed in China through Colorcraft Ltd., Hong Kong

PRAISE FOR *WHAT MUSIC MEANS TO ME*

"THOUGH every photo of the music-loving faces in *What Music Means to Me* speaks its proverbial 'thousand words,' the book's musicians also express their musical passion in their own loving language. Combined with author Richard Rejino's artfully executed images, these personal statements make the magic of music come alive, reflecting its pleasure, its healing, its inspiration and its connection to the divine. *What Music Means to Me* leaves an unforgettable imprint on the heart."

Laurel Fishman
Grammy.com music advocacy columnist, music/media specialist

"WITH stunning photos and startling personal essays, the truths of these musicians and of music itself are revealed. Read their words. Look into their eyes. A personal connection is made. You will visit them time and again. You will remember their names.

Richard has created a compelling compilation that will appeal to musicians and non-musicians alike. A warning to the non-musicians: after you enter their world, you might want to join it."

Tracy Begland
Dallas Morning News
Community Voices Columnist

"IT is a challenge to adequately express, in a few words, what I find so satisfying about this book. It is far easier to just pick it up and and look into the eyes of the stories you tell. They make visible what I often find difficult to understand or express – When music goes in, my spirit is nourished; and a better 'me' comes out."

Denny Senseney
Music Educator, Music Advocate & Music Merchant

"PHILOSOPHERS have tried for centuries to express the meaning of music. Through powerful photographs and poignant words, the subjects in *What Music Means to Me* have come as close as I've ever seen to describing the indescribable."

Joe Lamond
President, National Association of Music Merchants

"THROUGH striking photographs and compelling personal accounts, Richard Rejino captures not only the musician's passion, but the musician's soul. From the hearts of musicians, young and old, this wonderfully artistic book embodies the transformative power of music."

Paula Crider
Music Educator, Professor Emeritus, University of Texas

RICHARD REJINO

—————————————

WHAT MUSIC MEANS TO ME

WWW.WHATMUSICMEANSTOME.ORG

CONTENTS

I dedicate this book to my loving wife, Mona; for all of her

encouragement and support that she lovingly bestowed

during the journey of making this book.

She is my morning

light.

And

to my children,

Maggie and Adam; to show them

that finding a passion and following a dream

is a process that will lead you to discover who you really are.

AUTHOR'S NOTE & ACKNOWLEDGEMENTS

An art teacher once said to me that kids in school today have everything they want instantaneously; they don't have to wait long for anything. At the click of a mouse, students can do their homework, chat with friends, listen to music and watch YouTube simultaneously! She said, "What they are missing in education is the art of process."

Indeed, process is at the very heart of music and all the arts. It would be impossible to learn the Beethoven "Waldstein Sonata" by looking it up on the internet or by listening to a recording. You can't paint a masterpiece when you color by numbers, nor can you write a novel in a day. It takes time.

When learning music, it requires that you delve into it and into yourself to build a representation of what the music means to you. We toil in the details, but ultimately listen to ourselves to interpret the music as only we can. During this process, we are given much needed time to reflect and learn more about what we are made of, to allow ideas to ferment, to ripen. Taking time allows us to evolve and see the world differently so that we can bring our truest and most honest selves to the music. In doing so, it changes our perspective and we are the wiser for it.

The "What Music Means to Me Project" (WMMTMP) is the culmination of the "art of process" that the art teacher said was missing from our kids' education. Two years in the making, the WMMTMP was created to raise public awareness of the benefits of music in our education and in the quality of life. Through the use of photographic images and personal statements, the project gives a voice to music students, teachers, professionals and the impact music has had in their lives.

My hope is that this book will encourage others to make music and enhance their lives through it; to encourage school administrators to keep music in schools; to, in some small way, bring music and all the arts closer to the center of our lives. By extension, this project has been one of the most rewarding experiences of my life and it has been my privilege to photograph these inspiring individuals and be the messenger of their stories.

An undertaking of this kind could not have been possible without the help, guidance and encouragement of many trusted friends and colleagues. From the beginning I have been blessed with both, each of whom has given much of their time and of themselves to help make this project a reality. I will remain forever grateful and moved by your contributions. In particular, I want to thank Madeleine Crouch who lit the fire under me to pursue the idea of "What Music Means to Me" many months ago; Karen Austin and Toni Austin-Allen who helped me find my footing early on in the process of recruiting and photographing subjects; Ed Long, of the Hockaday School, Brenda Dillon, Carol Leone, Carmen Doubrava, Marcy McDonald, and Judith Pruitt for finding enthusiastic and wonderful students that were willing to participate in this project; Tracie Fraley, principal, Bart Marantz and Kent Ellingson, teachers, at the Booker T. Washington High School for the Performing and Visual Arts, for allowing me to use your campus as a backdrop for your extraordinary students; Pat Thompson, also of Booker T. Washington, for making it all happen with such good cheer and patience, and Jamie Allen for helping me get my foot in the door; the people at the DSO for allowing me to use the fantastic light in the lobby of the Meyerson Symphony Center; and Walter Eagleton whose experience and advice helped me with the challenges of photographing on location.

A special thanks to the awe-inspiring Brian Chung whose magnificent piece of prose introduces this humble book; and to Barbara Kreader, my friend, sounding-board and biggest cheerleader in this project, for your insight and beautiful poetry, a prelude to each chapter.

Finally, to my wife, Mona, a friend, confidant, an angel, and to my splendid children, Maggie and Adam; thank you for helping me remain true to my vision. You give me love, and therefore, you give me courage.

Richard Rejino
Carrollton, Texas

FOREWORD
BY
BRIAN CHUNG

You are about to explore a world of immense and irrepressible power.

With such an introduction, one might expect this book to examine the rise of Western imperialism in the postmodern world or the brutish realities of Soviet repression under Stalin. Failing that, it could at least offer a retrospective on the mighty Green Bay Packers dynasty under Vince Lombardi. But no—not even Donald Trump or Hillary Clinton merit a scant reference here.

Such examples of personal and ideological power are captivating, but often transitory. Political regimes and sports dynasties rise and fall. Business and cultural luminaries come and go. But amid these pages flows a power that is both cogent and enduring—one that seldom makes headlines, but has a greater capacity to enrich the very soul of our society than all the above combined. Such is the prodigious power of music making.

Admittedly, some may scoff at the notion that so genteel a form of expression could be a force so formidable. After all, one can only imagine how the Philadelphia Orchestra might fare in a street brawl with the Green Bay Packers. But brute force is only one limited form of power. When viewed through the lens of human potential, power reveals itself as inspiration, encouragement, impact—the ability to not just control others, but to transform them productively and profoundly from the inside out. This is the mind-stretching, life-altering kind of power that those who make music have experienced since the dawn of man.

Birth of Rock

I wasn't actually there, but it's safe to assume that music making started at the beginning— perhaps when caveman Gog discovered that pounding one stone against another in rhythmic fashion lighted up his senses. One envisions a giddy Gog sprinting to his buddy Nog's cave to pound out his latest rhythmic creation of early rock. Not to be outdone, Nog starts banging his club against a hollow tree trunk while throwing in a few gratuitous grunts (Snoop Nog begets rap?). Eventually, grunts give way to melodies; sticks and stones give way to phrases and tones—and a wondrous new world of music making is born.

It isn't long before music making captures the imagination of cave dwellers everywhere who discover they are wired to make music. Music lets them express feelings when primitive utterances fail. It arouses their minds to think beyond the banalities of daily life. It brings fun and camaraderie to dreary Saturday nights without cable. It offers a welcome, soothing respite from the stresses of all-too-frequent T-Rex sightings. In short, it invigorates every facet of life—and has done so for a long, long time.

Music for Moderns

As music making has evolved across the millennia, so has its impact on the life of man. Today, it could be argued that music making circumnavigates a life. It does its edifying work *on* us, *in* us, *around* us, *through* us—and the lives it touches are never the same.

You'll see this in the pages that follow. Music making introduced John not only to his first love but to his true self. It transported Grace from the rice fields of Communist China to the classrooms of California. It persuaded Olmar to leave home, family and security in pursuit of a dream. It gave Jonathan a way of escape from the perils of gang violence. It offered April, a musical novice at age 32, a new and fulfilling career. It helped Dennis find healing after the loss of his 23-year-old son. Again and again, the power of music making changes lives.

But perhaps most compelling is its power to bring lives together. In a 1998 essay, writer Anne Lamott* described a "miracle" that occurred at her church as music somehow united two congregants who were socially and morally divided. There seemed to be no way to bridge the chasm between them. Yet, it was music that brought them together—standing side-by-side in the pew, reduced to uncontrollable tears, holding each other up, surrendered to a newfound understanding of grace, love and forgiveness. "I can't imagine anything else but music that could have brought about this alchemy," Lamott writes. "How is it that you have a chord here and another chord there… and then your heart breaks open? I don't know the answer. Maybe it's because the music is about as physical as it gets. Your essential rhythm is your heartbeat; your essential sound the breaths. We're walking temples of noise. And when you add the human heart to this mix, it somehow lets us meet on a bridge we couldn't get to any other way."

How do we comprehend such power? Perhaps it's not so important that we do. Maybe all that really matters when it comes to music making is that all of us—those who play and those who don't—come to a fuller realization of all that it **does**, and never fail to treasure what it **is:**

> … a gift of God (Luke)
> … a sanctuary (Tiger)
> … a never-failing friend (Olmar)
> … the highest influence in this
>   modern age (Jonathan).

Or, as Elvia puts it simply… "Making music is the most wonderful thing in the world."

*Lamott, Anne. "Knockin' on Heaven's Door." This American Life (November 21, 2008). Podcast available at: http://www.thisamericanlife.org/Radio_Episode.

What Music Means to Me

Music as Joy

I am music!
Delight in me.

Fling your guitar on your back.
Cradle your viola in your arms.
Follow me.

Whether you are alone
in an empty white room
or in front of a roaring crowd,

I will make light dance in your eyes,
lift the burden from your shoulders,
bring you a lifetime of joy.

I am music!

Lewis

When I play the piano, I feel like I'm in an empty white room. It's a place where I am alone with God. I just hear myself playing as harmonies and melodies run from my head to my fingers. The main thing I love about the piano is bringing out the emotion when I play. For some reason I have a natural ability to share the same feelings with people. Playing the piano soothes me and I always feel refreshed after I practice. God really helps with that. I just play for Him and feel even more amazed about what He has given me. Playing the piano is also fun to me for many reasons. I like to perform in competitions and encourage other young artists. I love writing my own songs and making my own arrangements. It surprises me sometimes when I'm just doodling around and come up with the most wonderful music I've ever played in my life! Sometimes I hear songs in my head that are so complicated that I can't even write or play what I hear. It's amazing what I can do. I really wouldn't know where to go without music or God. *Music is law free* – I can play whatever I feel or think. It's a great feeling!

Josh

"Words make you think a thought. Music makes you feel a feeling. Songs make you feel a thought." –unknown

I cannot fathom any experience more cathartic than lifting an intangible burden off my shoulders by meshing words with music—creating a piece of art that equals more than just the sum of its parts. The only experience that could even come close is sharing this creation with others. It is an incredible phenomenon that one person can make an entire room of strangers privy to the esoteric feelings he once felt when he was stringing these phrases together.

I'll never forget my first experience sharing a song I wrote with an audience. It was my first summer at Camp Sabra, in Rocky Mountain, Missouri. I had worked the entire session at camp perfecting my song, an ode to the joys of the summer camp experience. On the last night of camp, during the ever-nostalgic closing campfire, I got the opportunity to perform my song for all 400 campers and staff. After the camp director led everyone in all the traditional campfire musical fare, he called me up to sing my original. Hot blood coursing through my veins, I approached the microphone, my guitar gaining a pound with each step I took. I introduced the song, started playing the opening pentatonic riff. I messed up a few notes, but the audience didn't seem to care – they were already clapping along to the rhythm! I jumped into the first verse, "It's a cool night in Missouri, sittin' by the fire…" The crowd roared. By the time I got to the chorus for the third time, I heard hundreds of voices singing my words along with me—the ultimate compliment for any songwriter. I played the closing plagal cadence, and the audience burst out into cheering. I heaved a great sigh of relief, and couldn't stop a huge half moon smile from waxing across my face. All of my writing, rewriting, and practice finally paid off—I was finally a bona fide songwriter. I hope to continue honing my skills as a singer, musician and songwriter for the rest of my life.

Shabria

I remember a time when music was not a big part of my life. That was a time where I felt like I had nothing to live for. I was on the path of becoming a pediatrician, a career that was brought onto me, and I knew that I didn't have a passion for it. I followed this career path because I was told to do so at the age of 7 and by a former viola teacher. She told me to "give up viola and become a doctor," and that is exactly what I did.

Three years ago my heart brought me to play viola again, and my passion from that day forward will never fade. I love playing viola because it gives me a sense of empowerment. I love the fact that I didn't let someone stop me from pursuing my true dream and that I overcame the negativity to get to where I am today. Every time I go on stage and look at the blinding spotlight and hear the roaring crowd, I feel extremely blessed to have this opportunity, and I honestly wish that every child will get the opportunity to play music.

Playing music has taken me all over the United States and sooner or later all over the world. I do not think that anyone should let someone tell them that they cannot play music. If anything, learn from my mistake and keep going; no one can take your dream away. I know that I will play the viola for the rest of my life and that music to me, means a lifetime of joy!

Monique

Music is not something that you do, it is something that you are because it consumes you and won't let go—ever. It's the piece of your life that will be empty if you decide to divorce it. I say divorce because once you start it you love it, you are married to it. It is not something that you can have an affair with, you have to love it unconditionally. I am married to music and my music is married to me. It will never leave me nor forsake me, it won't lie to me at any point; either it's great or it royally sucks. It is the thing that holds the pieces of everything that surrounds me together. My definition of music is the peace it gives me and the strength that holds my life. My definition does not have the words of theory because I don't see it as something that you can learn but something that you know and feel.

Music is me and I am Music.

What Music Means to Me

Music as Passion

I excite passion.

Meet me eye to eye.
Drop your coat.
Give up your home.

Use me to break
the boundaries
of your imagination.

Music – yes! Open your heart to me.

Olmar

Two years ago, I was lucky enough to attend a summer high school musical institute. Attending the institute was my first opportunity to experience collegiate-level studies in music and explore my options in music as a career. Unfortunately, when I returned home to Dallas, my newfound excitement was challenged; when I told my grandparents that I wanted to pursue a career in music, they were less than thrilled.

In my grandparents' culture, careers in music are not the most respected. My grandparents would rather see me as a lawyer or doctor; someone of "importance." In addition, I attended Booker T. Washington High School for the Performing and Visual Arts, which obviously did not go over well with them. In fact, this upset my grandparents so much that they threatened to withdraw me and enroll me in a comprehensive high school. I could not let this happen.

On the first day of my junior year, a day when everyone is excited to see their friends after a long summer, I dealt with my grandparents taking me out of Booker T. Washington. From that moment on, I knew that day was going to change the rest of my life. I did the impossible and left home, becoming homeless to pursue my future in music. Fortunately, I knew many families who would help me overcome my obstacles. During a period of four months, from couch to couch, I lived in four different homes, all while getting through my academically challenging junior year of high school.

Hardships occur in each of our lives, and I fully realized that no one's life is perfect. I did not let the difficulties in my life get me down; I knew that nobody would believe in me unless I believed in myself. Even though I was not living with my grandparents, I wanted to make them proud of me and be the first person in my family to graduate from high school and to attend college. As the months passed, I kept asking myself: "Why are you doing this? Is this all worth it?"

I answered my own questions during my first opera show with my high school's Opera Workshop class performances. I sang "Vecchia zimarra, senti" from *La Boheme*, the coat aria – it was the first time I had ever been able to throw myself fully into a character while singing. When I dropped my coat at the end of my aria, I had a sudden epiphany – the coat symbolized my home. I gave up my home, my family, and my security to pursue my career in opera, just like Colline gave up his prized possession to buy Mimi medicine. I felt magic tingling throughout my mind and body, making me dizzy with happiness. I knew then I had made the right decision.

Ever since then, I have never stopped listening to and performing music. No matter what I'm going through, I can always rely on music to remind me of the true beauty in life. Music has always been able to comfort and calm me in times of trouble. I would consider music to be more than passion – it's more like a never-failing friend.

Biliana

I often think about what made me the person I am today and I always find the same answer— it has been my parents and playing the piano.

It wasn't until fifteen years ago when my first student made me realize I didn't have memories from the time before music came into my life. I grew up in Sofia, Bulgaria. My mother is a concert pianist, and my father is an engineer – "the only quiet person in the family of musicians" as he always jokes. I started playing the piano at the age of five. At seven, I was accepted at the National Music School from which I later graduated. Later, I went to the Conservatory in Sofia and upon graduation as a Piano Performance Major I came to the US. I was 21, I was by myself and I had $200 in my wallet and two big suitcases.

Music makes me feel like I always have something to discover and something to learn. It enriches my personality. With each piece I find a new trait in my character which I was not aware of before; something I can recreate in my own way, every time from a different perspective.

Music teaches me discipline and consistency, it breaks the boundaries of my imagination. It improves my concentration. Playing helps me find the meaning behind the notes, a privilege very few people can achieve. Music is what makes me a very emotional and sensitive person, it helps me express my feelings better. Sometimes after a bad day I just need to listen to a slow movement of a Rachmaninoff piano concerto to help me start crying and then to recover from it. I cannot think of anything else that would make me feel the same way but music.

Music is like beauty, so pure and absolute. It helps me strive for perfection. At least to get as close to it as I possibly can. It makes me a better person with higher standards. Nothing keeps me going every day better than striving for perfection. Music makes me more sincere and honest. When I perform a piece I open my entire heart to it and I feel like I can be more myself than ever. I strive for the same in my personal relationships. Music never disappoints me, but people do sometimes.

Music influences every aspect of my life. I cannot imagine living without it. It completes me, the part of me that nothing else can complete.

Annie

Passion is a strong word that can take on different forms. Whether the form is love or hate or joy or sorrow, it is a driving force inside the human soul that brings about everything, from art to war. It is a result of great passion. However, passion does not always have to be a huge war to change the world. It has been said, "If you change yourself, you change the world." The passion inside drives these changes, and my goal is to change the world with my passion: music.

People allow their emotions to be affected by the music they listen to and this vulnerability places a great deal of responsibility on the musicians. Songs can alter people's perspectives on different subjects. There have been stories of people on the verge of emotional and mental collapse who claim that a song literally saved their life. One night after one of my shows, a girl around 16 years old came up to me. She expressed that my song, *Crash*, had given her hope. The line, "to crash is the only release," spoke to her and told her that sometimes it is necessary to hit rock bottom to be able to rise again. Music is powerful. Musicians have been given the gift of this responsibility. Songs can change the world. I can change the world.

Music is my passion. I cannot escape it. It is a part of who I am. It has strengthened my understanding of people and their emotions. I have come to realize that music is my calling in life and it must be nurtured correctly to be able to grow and change the world.

Melodies draw people in; the lyrics keep them listening. It is my responsibility to use my gift to change the world one audience at a time. Whatever the feeling, I will use my music to guide, relax, entertain, evoke emotion, give peace, cause reflection, give hope, bring a smile, and perhaps, lift a burden.

"I am a warrior, guarding the innocent and fighting battles that aren't always mine. And I am a storyteller, keeper of the words that bind together generations of time."
–*Internal Wonder*, Annie

What Music Means to Me

Music as Wisdom

I evoke wisdom.

With bow raised high, senses tuned,
you call me a force.

I soothe beasts, unite people as one.

From the lips of your wry smile,
you say I give peace.

I entertain, sustain and guide you.

In clasped hands you hold me up
as your experience of mortality
spun in real time.

Body arched in unison with the piano,
you insist I can make or break dreams.

With strong arms folded, you claim
you can create me from anything.

You bring me to life. I am music.

Thor

I think that without music in my life, I would be little more dull as a person. I think I would be looking for other outlets of expression—I don't know if those would be good or bad. Having music in my life makes me more expressive, more complex, but also more open to a lot of different things. I view things in a different way than I usually would because with music you have to always be thinking about a deeper meaning: what someone was feeling when they wrote this, how did they come up with this. So, life in general is like music. The birds chirping, people moving, it all flows. All music is inspired from something, it had to have come from somewhere, some feeling, or some emotion, some part of life. I think that you can look around and you can make music from anything. You can sit outside and see nature: the water, the air, birds chirping. Then you can just as easily go down to Starbucks and see people moving and interacting. It's just like notes of a piece of music.

Music has given me a greater appreciation for life in general. Seeing how things work, being able to decipher the feeling of everything in life. It's all just like music, an expression. I have a greater appreciation for all other art forms because they are just like music: an expression of thought and of people's views of life. For me, music gives me an opportunity to express what life and all its complexities is like. There is no other way to do that.

Marcus

Music took me by surprise really. There I was sitting in a cramped audience of rambunctious third graders. I stared at the then mammoth and mystifying instrument—the cello. As a tiny hunched man emerged from the puke green curtains of the stage and addressed the inquisitive youth before him, he spoke of music. Eventually, he made his way to the cello that he made look minute, hunched over it and began to play.

From the opening chord his tone mystified me; I was the snake he was charming. His virtuosity, his passion appealed to me and my soul danced to the tarantella rhythm. Serpent-like and quick his hand moved up and down the fingerboard making screeching sounds, making melodies, making music. I began to ponder how one reached this new fantastical world of music and what it offered. The guest cellist's passion overflowed and his vivaciousness mingled with my curiosity and from that moment, I knew music was my passion.

Between each note, each phrase exists a secret— different for each person. Music for me is subdued passion manifested out of necessity. It completely floods my body and takes me to depths and heights of emotions that without music can only be imagined. Growing up as an only child, I confided in my instrument; my instrument has consoled me many times, it has helped me through life's low points and it has celebrated with me at times. Music gives me a reason to live... I wake up each day humming. We're inseparable. The ability of music to open up one's senses, change the way we view the world and at the same time teach us of the past is a profound tool. It has the ability to soothe beasts and bring people together. Music is the utmost expression of the complexities of feeling. And audience members, whether classically trained musicians or classical music virgins can FEEL what the music is describing.

Making music is a delicate art...you are given a blank canvas to which you add your touch, your emotions, your experiences and the rapport between the performer and the composer is what music is all about. It's very philosophical but on some level the performer must connect with the composer, realise his/her intentions and come to a compromise. This is how a piece sounds different played by each person... we don't all feel the same way.

Just as each person views colours differently, each person feels differently, loves differently, emotes differently. Because of this music has given me the ability to be empathetic. I can mentally and emotionally place myself in someone else's shoes and understand him/her better. It's the same thing that unites people. Emotions are universal, therefore music is as well.

Jonathan

"The Ability to Make Music Is The Ability to Influence."

We are influenced by other people, whether it's musically, politically or religiously. I believe that MUSIC is the highest influence in this modern age. The Ability to make music is the ability to influence. It can Make or Break our dreams, all depending on the Quality of Music.

Luke

The feeling one gets when participating in the act of creating music is a feeling like none other. One feels love, hate, joy, sadness, tranquility, distress all at once. I believe that this feeling is a gift from God: it is like a small taste of the feelings that God had when he created the universe, or when he creates a human being, an animal or a flower. Because when one makes music, especially in improvised music, they are giving life to ideas and feelings that are already inside of themselves. Keith Jarrett refers to this as building a world, taking everything that is inside of you and creating your own universe.

This is one of the most joyful experiences that a human being can have. However, it is not lasting simply because the life that is given in this act is also death. Music is created in time and through time, therefore, once an idea is given life, it is first presented and then it passes away forever. This is why the emotions that make up this feeling are so mixed, because we are ultimately experiencing our mortality in the life span of a piece of music.

I believe that music is so much more than just notes and rhythms, I believe that it is something that can truly help people and bring people together. I am not always very well understood when it comes to orally expressing myself; however with music, I find that the feelings and the beliefs that are inside of me come out more clearly and poignantly than I could have ever expressed in words. Music is truly a universal language and with it you can express to the world everything that is inside of you.

I feel blessed beyond measure to have been allowed to experience this feeling and I believe that God has allowed me to experience it so that I can see His will for my life; to bring others to Him through my music. Therefore, through music, God has given my life purpose.

Music as Healing & Wellness

I welcome you home to yourself.

Bring your wide-eyed vulnerability to me.
Write your story using my pitches and rhythms
to sketch your pain.

Defy violence with your steely stare.
I will be your peaceful sword.
Use me to protect your right to a better life.

Speak through me.
Let me be the spark in your eyes,
the emotion that spills from your lips.

I live behind the scrolls of your antique music rack.
Liberate me. I will welcome your melancholy,
dance with your merriment.

Turn your curious ear to me.
Analyze my chords, cadences, arpeggios.
Lose yourself in the joy of my harmonies, melodies, rhythms.

I live on because your teacher
unleashes your unbounded energy,
shows you how to release me from the prison of the score.

Play with me. I will transform your grief,
pick up where your words leave off,
change your sober expression into a smile.

When the unattended piano calls to you,
answer it. Get distracted.
Dabble. Use me to match your mood.

I am music, your protector. I make you whole.

Riley

Music is my diary. . .

I've suffered from an eating disorder for almost eleven years of my life. It started when I was 7 years old. I think that a lot of people believe that people who have eating disorders choose to have them. But that's not true. My eating disorder chose me. Having an eating disorder is hard. I have all these feelings and I don't know how to read them sometimes. I've kept so many secrets, I've told so many lies. My eating disorder has consumed me. You may not be able to tell by my physical appearance that I have anorexia nervosa because, over the years, I've learned to maintain a healthy weight. But on the inside, I'm so lost.

Music is my diary. . .

I've been playing the piano for almost eleven years. I've never really been able to read music very well, but I have a really good ear. When I was younger, I would hear a song on the radio and sit down at my keyboard and play it. I spend hours playing the piano now in my free time. When I play, I can identify my feelings. I can just play my feelings on the piano. When I play, all of my troubles disappear for a moment and Riley shines through. Because of music, I have found myself.

Music is my diary . . .

Jonathan

Music gives me a feeling of purpose in this world. I feel like I belong for once in my life. No matter what race or social status you may be, music allows you to feel a sense of unity. When I sing in the choir, or even when I sing solos, I feel as though I am connected to this entirely new world of music beyond anyone's understanding, beyond any earthly feelings.

I grew up in one of the roughest environments of Dallas. Every night there were either gun shots or people arguing in the streets. This was a struggle for me as a young man knowing that one day that could be me causing all the noise, keeping innocent children awake.

My life before music was to just live for the thrill of trouble. Music saved me from a life of trouble and heartache. I don't have to worry about going to jail or getting involved in gangs, because I was given an escape through my music. I've learned that I can live a life full of joy and prosperity no matter where I live or grew up. Music gives me the confidence to say "no" to peer pressure put on me every day. I can now look at my surroundings as an inspiration to live a better life, not only for me, but for my future children.

Ben

Music, a therapeutic method of healing, is used to give the mute a voice and to give the mentally disabled a new life.

Before I engaged deeply into music, I considered myself a mute, one without the ability to communicate my thoughts and meaning. As I immersed myself into the musical world, I began to see the beauty of rhythm and melody with every experience I encountered. I started to see life from a different perspective: as if the world were just an on-going movie scene. Music began to play in my head and original tunes formed endlessly as the day went on. Gradually my life began to seem more colorful and lively.

Music gave me the spark I needed to run throughout the day with a little kick to my step, a twinkle in my eye, a cherry on top. Music is what gives me the a reason for being, what softly wakes me up in the morning, what gently tucks me in at night. Music flows through my veins and into my soul, the very essence of music pulsates in my blood and gave me a new life.

No longer am I this once muted shell, but now an invigorated flurry of emotion and life. Music, a beam of light, brightens the life of every individual that encounters and understands the passion and emotion spilled in the piece because, "Artists must be sacrificed to their art. Like bees, they must put their lives into the sting they give." –Ralph Waldo Emerson

Joyce

No one knows that no matter how long
I've ignored her, my piano welcomes the
prodigal me home.

No one knows that when I am alone,
surrounded by a world of others, she is
a welcomed companion to my chosen
solitude.

No one knows how she consoles me in my
unwelcome melancholy and dances with me
in my desired merriment.

No one knows how carefully she listens to
my fingers and gives them loving voice.

No one knows how she responds with joy
when my touch is successful and how sadly
morose she becomes when it is not.

No one knows my piano has a life of her
own and is my secret, always reliable friend.

Skip

A lifelong research physicist by training, I have an innate curiosity of how and why things work. Many times I wished for the ability to create or interpret a piece of piano music with feeling; to achieve the dynamic levels, the subtle variances in timing, in attack to make each note sound as if caressed in its forming. The ethereal quality of Leon Fleisher playing J.S. Bach's *Sheep May Safely Graze* comes to mind as a goal worth a lifetime of pursuit.

I gave up a profession that I truly loved to move to Texas. Much of my career and passion was in the secret world of modern armor design and development for the Army's fighting vehicles. I had always 'used my head' solving some technical or theoretical problem associated with work.

Salvation came in the form of beginner group piano lessons. Here was a chance to start from the beginning learning about triads and arpeggios and building chords and progression of chords and cadences and subtleties in creating even a single note.

Like research, this endeavor is ever expanding, with new knowledge and bright colors and hues and seemingly magic complexities. And, like research, time and hard work is required. I graduated to private lessons and found each lesson exciting and akin to what a master class must be like. I have read Stuart Isacoff 's *Temperament*, Seymour Bernstein's *With Your Own Two Hands*, Thad Carhart's *The Piano Shop On the Left Bank* and James Barron's *Piano – The Making of a Steinway Concert Grand*. I recommend their reading to every piano student.

Nine months ago, my wife, Ann and I bought a factory restored 1923 Steinway Model O Grand. Practicing becomes so self-absorbing that time has no meaning. Often an hour or two passes by without my realization. I am lost in the joy of harmony and rhythm and melody.

I told my teacher a few months ago that she had "saved my retirement." Certainly I had always appreciated and been emotionally moved by good music, but I was always an observer and never a participant. Now I am a student of that marvelously complex instrument—the piano—with the nearly infinite variations of sound quality and music it can be made to create. Never mind that it will take five or ten or twenty years to achieve some level of proficiency, it will be a continuing source of challenge and great joy in my life. I feel so blessed to now have the time to do this.

Caroline

As I stood in the house where I took ten years of piano lessons, the very same house where I grew to love this woman, it dawned on me how much of my life had been shaped by her.

I had received an invitation to a house party to be held at my former piano teacher's house; she had redesigned, remodeled, and redecorated parts of her house, somewhat concurrent with my piano lessons. This was the first time I visited her home studio in over a year, for I had taken a parent-generated "sabbatical" from lessons. I have often wished my parents did not doubt my ability to handle the pressure of being an enthusiastic and avid student, a Drum Major at school, and a musician – but I had in truth forsaken my weekly piano lessons.

My lessons with Carmen began after years of admiring my older sister Afton's piano playing. Whether she was any good didn't concern me, not that I could tell anyway. What excited and exhilarated me was the music. I would sit-in on her lessons so that I could listen to Carmen play or tell Afton what to do with the paper music to transform it into soulful music – the music that causes you to reminisce about a person or place, that makes your heart break every time you hear it, or that causes you to crack a smile. I wanted the ability to evoke such emotions and reactions, and Carmen created in me that want.

Every Sunday for ten years, one hour of my life was spent in the studio at Carmen's house: playing piano, learning theory, and developing as an individual. The pictures she shared of her trips across the U.S. incited in me an urge to travel. Shared global concerns and her investments in healthier living, years prior to any "green" campaign, initiated my interest in an alternative lifestyle.

It wasn't just the music that I played, but it was also Carmen's presence in my childhood that calcified my confidence and strength in being myself. Though it takes many more years than I have lived to develop a person, Carmen has unknowingly given a hand in building my foundation.

Casey

When my Uncle passed away, it was a shock to our family. I turned to music right away because the others around me were so consumed with grief that I felt out of place; I was too young to know him as well. I began composing and I wrote four pieces alone in that first week. I played the second movement of the Beethoven *Pathetique* for my grandmother every day because she didn't want to speak with anyone and, having been a piano teacher herself, could only relate to music for a long time. Playing and composing will probably always be linked to my family because of my Uncle's passing now, but I don't think that's a bad thing; my family will always be my greatest pride and my greatest accomplishment, so combining my family and my music will probably improve both things in the long run.

Music has always been what picks up where my words leave off. I have the tendency to say the wrong thing when using words, but music can never be wrong to me. Wrong notes, sure, but that's just like stuttering or spoonerisms. Music itself can never be wrong and I feel like it's the one great string linking me to every other person I see. Every day, every second in my life has theme music and everyone I encounter contributes to it. Every moment of my life is a symphony and sometimes I don't even have to say a word.

Christine

I like that people have a relationship with a piano—one that will never get old and no one can take away. I can express myself without saying a word. I play more often when I'm sad or angry than when I'm happy. Music making calms me whenever I'm stressed or gives me something more interesting to do than watching TV or surfing the web. Everything slows down when I play. All I think of is the emotion the composer wanted to evoke. I play a combination of the piece's emotion and my own. I know that someone else, the composer, has felt the same way. There's comfort in that.

There's also something about an unattended piano; it calls to me. It gives me a lot of confidence and a sense of accomplishment whenever I memorize a piece fully and polish it. I think you can sometimes tell a lot about a person by the way they play a piece or the pieces they choose. In a way, I'm a bit of a spontaneous and sentimental spirit, so when I sit down to practice one piece I usually get distracted and dabble on pieces I've played in the past or change from classical to jazz or contemporary. It's amazing how you can match a piece to fit your mood anytime you want.

Candace

Throughout my high school years I struggled with clinical depression and at one point was hospitalized. There have been times when I did not think I was going to make it through. I felt like I was the only person in the world having these feelings.

Music, however, gave me a connection to people that I would not have had otherwise. Through my music and the music of others, I am part of a family of clever, deep, and passionate people. I came to see that I was not alone, and also that there is no pain without purpose. These people and their music showed me how to be part of something greater than myself and how to express my feelings creatively.

At times I have questioned the menacing competition in the field of music, but the infinite power of music transcends all finite human discord. Victor Hugo once said that "music expresses that which cannot be said and on which it is impossible to be silent." I have been through ups and downs with my violin, consistent with the emotional ups and downs. But music remains that symbol of hope and sometimes just enough magic to inspire me to keep struggling. Music is magic; it is what my soul sounds like.

What Music Means to Me

Music as Determination

I demand work.

Vibrate the strings with your bow.
Beat your drumsticks until they both blur.

Microphone near to your lips,
breathe and wail your voice into the world.

Marimba wood under your sticks
bring me alive in a pulse with your heart.

Sing – let your soul fly with me.

Trust yourself;
      labor to the brink of your capabilities;
           struggle;
               become stronger.

Live for me. I, music, live in you.

Elvia

Music has been a part of my life ever since I can remember. I started playing the violin in fourth grade just for fun, but as the years passed, my music has gotten me to different places and through different struggles.

I think that by playing my instrument, I have had to learn to balance my academics with my art. I have to study in order to get good grades in my classes and I have to practice too. It can be a challenge. I've had to stay up late at times, because I've had rehearsal and a major test I needed to study for too. I've learned to schedule my life and follow what I need to do in daily activities and in goals because of orchestra. I will plan out what I need to get done in a day, but I will also plan out what I want to achieve in life. I've become more organized.

Without my music or my instrument, I wouldn't be where I am now. Music has matured me and helps me in real situations. It has helped me accomplish my goals of attending the schools of my choice. Music has also opened doors towards new and great opportunities such as scholarships.

Music has matured me because I've learned to cooperate with others and I've also learned to depend on myself. As an orchestra member, I've learned that if there is no communication between the players, then a piece might not be as perfect as if there was communication. The same applies to every day things. Communication is key to many things. When I play my solos I've learned to trust myself, because I am the only one that is capable of helping me. This helps me feel independent.

Making music is the most wonderful thing in the world. I admit that sometimes it can be exhausting. Performing in front of strangers while my legs are shaking with fear is not a blast, but the outcome of playing, having people congratulate me and being proud of myself, is worth everything and more.

Austin

About the time of seventh grade I became extremely serious about music. I started to ignore other aspects of life that I had thought of as essential, such as computer games, being popular, fitting in, TV, and more.

I love to practice. I work as hard as I can to learn everything possible about the music in front of me, and after I have learned it to a point where I feel comfortable, it is great to reflect that not too long ago, this was a new and seemingly difficult piece. The effort is half the fun because I know that I am becoming a better musician with every note, every strike, every hit.

When I play music, I feel a sense of ease and comfort. It is as if I am channeling something much larger than myself. I am sometimes able to just look down at myself and feel a sense of awe that I am creating all of these sounds and textures. I love to feel myself creating music.

When people ask me what I like to do, the answer that comes most readily to mind is music. Through music, I have trained myself to work to the brink of my capabilities. I have trained myself to have discipline, organization, time management, and an overall sense of perseverance. If there is a task ahead of me, due to my musical experience, I am not afraid to face it no matter how daunting it may seem. I believe that music is a part of me, it is me, and I am it.

Anna

Music making has not always been an easy thing for me. Sometimes piano playing has been an up and down pursuit since the pieces can be so hard to learn and play well. When I was assigned Ravel's *Piano Concerto in G*, though I loved listening to it, I was sure I could not play it. What I learned is that music making sometimes takes me on journeys that I never would have imagined to be possible.

I have always wanted to play a concerto with a symphony orchestra. What I have noticed is that many capable pianists never get the opportunity. I looked for opportunities for more than a year, taking it to several competitions, determined to find something but without success. One unlikely opportunity came with the Lewisville Lake Symphony Competition. The Ravel concerto was not even on their list of approved pieces, but I got permission to audition with it anyway. Needless to say, I wasn't too hopeful. I played the best I could, and found to my amazement that I was actually one of the two Grand Prize winners and that I would further get to play with the Lewisville Lake Symphony! This was an amazing dream come true for me, an experience I will never forget.

Music has taught me that it's okay to dream and struggle, and that hard work and persistence pay off in the end.

Jazzmeia

"Music is noise organized in time; it is also a form of art. Music is a normal part of my life. Music can be a way to open or touch someone's heart through and through. Music can be used spiritually to make it through rough times. Music Lives in me."

I am a student at Booker T. Washington High School for the Performing and Visual Arts where I study as a Jazz Vocalist Major and I have crossed clustered to a Visual Artist as well. It took time, perseverance, motivation, inspiration and determination to attend Booker T. The first two times that I auditioned I was not accepted. I thought about giving up. I told myself that I'd never audition again. One of the music directors told me that I did not have a classical background. I was told that my voice was too jazzy.

At the end of my sophomore year, I auditioned again – and I was accepted. I realized that perseverance was a weapon that I used to fight that battle, but the war was not over. I also realized that if I would have given up, I would not have had an opportunity to become stronger. That was an obstacle that I overcame that made me a better vocalist. Roger Boykin once said: "Anything you do that expands your mind makes you a better musician."

My deepest desire is to become a vocalist that can sing fine music; but also to read, teach, and play it just as well. Although I have been told that I show deep emotion and enthusiasm while singing, I just open my mouth and sing.

Meredith

I was in the Orff drum group at my middle school and when I came to the Hockaday School I missed it so much because there was nothing like it here. You either had choir or orchestra and that was it. So, my mom was working in the lower school and I would hang out there all the time. I'd see all these lower school Orff instruments that no one was using. I thought, hey, let's see if we can get something going. So, I started a small percussion group at the end of my sophomore year. There were about 15 of us and we'd play in the morning. I bought books and I started teaching songs and now it's grown to 40 people. We've got all this repertoire and we're a constant at ISAS and we got a standing ovation this year! It was so great!

The biggest difference I saw when I started the group was two things. I didn't really feel like I fit in. Once I started this percussion group I felt like I had a place in this school, I felt really, really connected to all the students. I was making my mark, my grades flew up. It connected me to the whole Hockaday experience. The second thing is that I LOVE seeing people coming in, new to the group, that have no musical skills—I'm talkin' they can NOT do it—and I'll work with them, I'll have tutoring sessions after school. By the end of the year they are rockin' out on the hardest parts. It's so gratifying for me to know that without that they wouldn't have been able to gain those skills. I know that I've impacted their lives in a significant way and that's really exciting for me. I've always seen myself being a teacher. I'm starting "Percussion for the Non-Percussionist" at Berklee next year!

Oneyda

As a child growing up it was kind of hard pursuing a career in music. I mean as a little kid it was cute, but as a teen still, dreaming the impossible was a joke to some of my family. In my family, at my age, I should already be working and have my head only inside a book. At least that's what one of my uncles decided to give comment on. Even to this day some of my family members criticize how I'm never home on the weekdays or on the weekends. I'm always gigging, in church singing, (as I have been for the last 10 years of my life), or in school rehearsing and getting educated. I can't help it though. I LIVE FOR MUSIC. I sing in church every Sunday thanking God for this wonderful and unique voice, as I offer it to him during mass. At first, even my Dad questioned himself on whether or not he should support me when I was accepted into Booker T.; he didn't want to see me disappointed if I never amounted to anything in the music industry.

I proved him wrong. I showed him how much I wanted it and he believed it. He saw my passion. He has seen my struggles, my ups, my downs, and triumphs. He actually showed me off to friends and family when I made the Texas All-State Women's Choir for the first time. He was proud. He saw me cry when other kids wouldn't talk to me because they saw me as a "teacher's pet" and a show-off in school and in church. He was saddened. My Dad sometimes tried to discourage me from singing just because he didn't want to see me hurt. But today he has nothing to doubt. After 17 years, I finally have my Dad actually believe in me. After 17 years, not one being on this earth has been able to keep me away from the wonders of music and I am sure no one ever will.

Music is my comfort, reality, and soul poured out on paper, a note, which becomes a pitch for the world to hear, feel, and live. Music not only creates images, color, and emotion but it unifies different cultures; it is a language. It gives a great example of how, in this world, all of us might be of a different race but we are one on the stage. On that stage, as one, the artists are the brain and decide whether they want to move a finger, shed a tear, laugh, dance, or simply tell a story. Music connects one person to another. I know. Awesome right? It's this feeling, this excitement that attracts me to music. One can influence and express in unimaginable ways that no scientist or schoolteacher can explain. It is only through experience that one can understand the ways of music yet, not even the best of all musicians is capable of explaining why. Music is magical. It's the only thing that brings meaning to life. This is what music means to me.

What Music Means to Me

Music as Sanctuary

I wrap you in sound.

Stand tall with your cello.
Let the strings' vibrations say all you cannot.

Gaze at your violin.
It speaks in sympathy with you when no one else can.

Eat and sleep with your guitar.
It teaches you about love, irony, heartbreak and glory.

Blow your deepest feeling into the hollows of your horn;
I will never betray you.

Lean on your piano in tough times.
Dream next to your clarinet.

Get excited about life.

I, music, will shelter your soul.

Tiger

Music is my sanctuary. A good piece of music has the ability to describe me better than any words can.

I don't want to say that music keeps me "sane," because in reality, what does sane even mean now? No one is completely sane, because then we would all be quite boring. What I will say is that music keeps me lucid. There is nothing that can transform my stress or horrible mood into such a state of placidity quite like music does.

It's amazing the transformation my mood makes even when I'm doing something as minute as holding a cake of rosin. I become filled to the brim with exhilaration upon pulling my bow across the strings of my cello, the sound of it resonating through the air around me, wrapping me up in a blanket, comforting me, putting me in a cocoon and sheltering me, even if only for a little while. The vibrations of the strings are my best way of conveying my emotions without having to use any words. My music can say what I cannot.

Music is what defines me. It has so many variations and complexities that I find it a compliment to say that music is the best way to show people who I am. Because I have difficulty showing emotions at times, I take pride in my music and try to share it with others as much as possible. I write music to get my point across to other people when I don't have words, because, as Stella Adler once said: "We are what we do, not what we say."

Music is everything to me.

Thao

When I was in first grade, my mother and father put me in a music class in school in downtown Dallas. This was where I began the violin. It was hard back then trying to learn the instrument. My family had just immigrated here from Vietnam. We barely had any money so my parents were always at work. Also, my family constantly moved around from place to place because my father was trying to get an education. It was difficult, and I think that's why I didn't like the violin at all back then. There were already so many problems, and along with that, my parents wanted me to take lessons and practice. First of all, I couldn't even keep a teacher because we moved around so much. Second of all, because I didn't have a teacher, I never made any progress, and I've always hated doing something I wasn't good at. However, no matter how much I protested, my parents forced me to play. So, everyday I would repeat the same song over and over again just to make them happy.

Eventually, things began to settle and the sun finally shined upon my family. My father completed his education and got a really good job as well as my mother, and I joined the orchestra at Ted Polk Middle School. It was amazing because I actually knew what was going on and the teachers told me that I was able to play really well. I felt amazing and began to do some real work with the violin based on that inspiration.

As the years went by, old problems settled and new problems rose. I guess that's the way life is, but there were moments where I felt I just wanted to be alone. Although I had many close friends, for some reason, I would just feel like being alone. The only thing there to comfort me then was music. It's actually pretty funny now that I think about it, but it seems as though music always understands how I am feeling. If I was in a bad mood, I would turn on the radio and a fugue would sympathize with me. If my mood was excitement, a finale to a symphony would be playing. I guess that's why I love the violin so much now. It's like my best friend because it can always understand how I feel and sympathize with me when no one else can.

Being able to play the violin gives me the ability to conjure up any friend I want at any given time in order to comfort myself. I appreciate what my mother and father have done when they forced me to play the violin everyday. If it weren't for that, I would not be where I am today. I would not be able to have the wonderful relationship with music as I do now.

Zach

There's that phrase, "Everything I ever needed to learn in life I learned from...," and people fill in the name of a significant parent, relative or teacher. My version would go, "Everything I ever needed to learn in life I learned from The Beatles."

I don't have my music time and my non-music time. If I'm not listening to an album, there's still a lyric, melody or rhythm swimming around in my head. If I'm not playing guitar, I'm still thinking up song ideas. While I enjoy the occasional silence, I will unconsciously put on an album, even at work in my career as a business magazine editor. This is not a sense I can turn off, just as it's not something I've turned on. I am not alone in this compulsion. For people like me, music is simply a part of our lifestyles. Perhaps this sounds extreme, even pathological to non-musicians and non-music lovers, but those who've been bitten by the bug understand: This is a part of us, no more bizarre or more unhealthy than eating and sleeping.

As such, music is also my all-encompassing philosophy and greatest teacher. Like many, I learned about love from The Beatles' "Abbey Road;" irony from Bob Dylan's "Blonde on Blonde;" heartbreak from Joni Mitchell's "Blue;" healing from Van Morrison's "Moondance;" passion from Derek and the Dominos' "Layla and Other Assorted Love Songs;" glory from Bruce Springsteen's "Born to Run;" the spiritual experience from U2's "The Joshua Tree;" and, more recently, the cycle of life from Wilco's "Sky Blue Sky."

There's more music out there than I will ever be able to hear. Sometimes, I'm afraid that I'll miss out on something great, but more often than not, I'm thankful that I've connected with this precious aspect of our world.

John

When I was young, I used to imagine what love would be like, how wonderful it would feel. I grew up with the idealized Hollywood picture in my mind of what my first love would be like. It would be gentle, kind, forgiving, comforting….unique.

As a kid, I was a bit nerdy and awkward. (Some would say this is still the case!) I was never much of a ladies' man. It's hard to be when you're short, scrawny and have glasses. So, I figured it would take a few years, or more, before I would be able to know what true love and passion were.

Yet in the seemingly most unattractive time of my life, love found me and grabbed me. I was in 6th grade and was introduced to my horn. It took a little while. I had to warm up to it. This love was a slow-developing love that needed to show me all that was possible through it. I found that I was able to express myself and all my emotions through my music.

Eventually, as I better learned the language of my love, I found that there were no limits to what I could do with it. I could confide my deepest feelings in it and not feel like it would betray me. I could show my happiness to it and it would rejoice with me. I could have a bad day and it would make it better. I could trust it when no one else was there. To say that music is more than just notes and rhythms is cliché. But there's a reason it's cliché. It's true.

Over the years, I have had girlfriends and I've married a wonderful person who has shared my love of music and has given me the world's most precious son.

I've known love in so many incarnations. My family, my friends, my dogs, my mentors, my students, my audiences. And while they are all dear to me, there's only been one that has always been by my side through everything in my life. It has seen the peaks of my happiness and has celebrated with me. It has also seen the valleys of my sadness and depression and has helped to pull me out. It has never left my side. When I had no one else, it was there. When I got married, it was there. When my wife was pregnant, it was there. When my beautiful son was born, again music was there. When my wonderful father-in-law lay dying, it was there to comfort him and those of us left behind.

There have been times that I've run from music because I was afraid of its sheer power. I was afraid of what it meant and what it took. But in trying to live without it, I found that I can never leave it behind. It isn't a part of me. It's been inside of me all along. What I've learned through it all is that this love of music is not something that is a separate entity from me. It is me.

Ana

At age twenty-four, I have a good idea of how wonderful or awful life can be, depending the path you choose. Many years ago, I chose music. To me it became my home. It doesn't matter where I live or who is around me, I know when I sit at the piano I am home, and I don't need to know more than that.

When I was in my country, the Dominican Republic, there was something I found very special in the fact that I played the piano. I loved it right away and it became my top priority since then. I loved playing piano, listening to music, reading about music. It became my addiction!

At home, we would have blackouts on a daily basis but, as a country dealing with such a situation for so many years, there were plenty of flashlights and candles around that allowed me to be at the piano. I always felt it was very special that no matter if there was electricity or not, I could still play!

Physical activities were limited to me after a major surgery when I was eight years old. I've been fully recovered since I was seventeen, but before that happened, it didn't become a tragedy or anything close to that. I was fully involved in music; I sang in choirs, played viola in orchestras, and the best of all, I played piano full time!

Regardless of the situation in my life, music is the one thing that keeps me going. When things get tough – and do they get tough! – I can turn to music. I cannot imagine what would be of me without it.

Molly

Music is both an intake and outlet of emotions. It has allowed me to convey a message when words weren't enough to help someone understand. When you let it fill you, the sound heightens all your senses, not just hearing, and lets the imagination take hold of you. I believe that it is a connecting point between this life and divinity.

Music can define a person's life and personality when you find the sort of music you are good at. It helps you find a core to yourself; a foundation that you can build your character on and around.

Jimmye

My mom put me in piano lessons as soon as I turned five. She was a big fan of Elton John and probably dreamed that someday, I'd be belting "Candle in the Wind" just for her. When I switched my instrument to the clarinet a few years later, I entered a general music competition at a Dallas church on a whim. It would be the first in a long and extensive line of competitions in which I did okay; they took me all over the world to compete and perform all throughout middle school and high school. Competitions were great in that they taught me how to cope with pressure and play with confidence, but win or lose, their outcomes never really mattered to me. It seemed like I was just building up a résumé and living to cater to judges; I never felt a real connection to my instrument or to the music. These sentiments changed during my junior year of high school during the first rehearsal with my local music ensemble, the Greater Dallas Youth Orchestra. I remember sitting there in silence, amazed by the intensity of the strings and bravado of the brass and winds and how the clarinet seamlessly weaved in and out, acting as just a small part of something much, much greater. I remember that incredible rush of energy, that excitement from being in the middle of all that sound and chords and notes and melody and thinking to myself, "This is how it's supposed to be." Ever since, I've looked at performance differently—it involves that translation of emotions between the audience and performer, a connection that has the potential to be endless.

Today, I am two weeks away from my high school graduation. While my class mates will be at a college studying everything from the earth's gravitational pull to Virginia Woolf's feminist ideals, I'll be learning how to fit triplets into a 9/8 time signature and ace the clarinet solo in Mahler's 5th. My mom never got me started in music lessons with the intention of making it my career. My decision to pursue music past grade school actually came just at the end of last year when I tried to imagine my life without a focus on music. I couldn't do it. I almost cried thinking about the possibility of never playing Brahms' *3rd Symphony* or never finishing Debussy's *Premiere Rhapsody*. And when I try to imagine the immense challenges ahead and the possibility of "never making it," but also the potential friendships, connections, and ultimate satisfaction that can result from music, I get excited. That's exactly what music gives me—it makes me excited about life.

MUSIC AS PROFESSION

Color the world with me.

Speak my language of emotion
to express your mood; alter your life.

Look for people who need my touch;
bring them humor, hope, strength and peace.

Smell the varnish of your viola;
tap its wood. Feel how I choose you.

Teach me to "all God's critters."
Relish that joy and privilege.

Experience the thrill of excellence.
Find me; it's never too late.

Discover yourself; bare your soul.
Look around you; appreciate all.

I am music. Make me yours.

Ann Marie

When meeting a person for the first time, there is a question I love to be asked: "What do you do for a living?"

Watching this new acquaintance's eyes light up when I say "I play in the Dallas Symphony" is almost as rewarding as a performance at the Meyerson. They smile, nod, and quite often reply "Oh, how wonderful. I LOVE music!"

I began playing the viola when I was in 4th grade. To be perfectly honest, when I signed up for strings class I had no idea what a viola was and was told by a wily salesman who had run out of violins, cellos and basses that I was much too tall to play the violin but still too small to play the cello. He put a viola under my chin and stretched my left hand around the scroll. "See?" he said, "it's a perfect fit." As it turned out it was a perfect fit and also the beginning of a long journey that would ultimately lead me to Dallas.

I remember taking my viola out of the case for the first time, brushing my fingers over the soft, fresh hair on the bow, plucking the strings and tapping the wood under my fingertips. It was glossy and smelled of new varnish, and I couldn't keep it out of my hands. I wanted so badly to play it, figure out how it worked, and how to translate the strange language on the page into real music. Each new note was a treasure to me, and stringing them together into a simple melody struck me as miraculous. I was completely smitten.

I was also terrible at it.

I am an incredibly stubborn human being. I chose music as my path not because I demonstrated any particularly stunning abilities from a young age but because I was bad at it. Playing the viola was challenging, mysterious and intriguing, and I wanted to play it well. As my mother so aptly put it, it kept

me "occupied." And so, the orchestra rehearsals, summer camps and private lessons began. With patient teachers and lots of practice I got better at playing and eventually went away to a special high school for the arts and completed my undergraduate and master's degrees from acclaimed conservatories. It was a long road filled with triumphs and disappointments, awards, defeats, and countless hours spent in practice rooms. And finally, one day over a decade ago, I came to Dallas to audition for the symphony. I have been here ever since.

A student recently asked me if I had it to do over again would I still pursue music as a career. I thought about it for a moment. I thought about the people that come to hear the symphony, my many teachers, mentors and coaches, and my cherished colleagues that I have been privileged to perform with for so many years. Would I do it over again? Absolutely.

I didn't choose music. It chose me.

Scott

I don't remember a time that I could not read music. I may have even learned to read music before I learned to read English. I really can't remember. Obviously I grew up in an environment surrounded by music. My mother was a piano teacher and taught me musical notation from a very early age. Both my mother and father were very musical. They were constantly listening to music or singing aloud whatever tune happened to be in their head at the time.

As an adult who makes his living performing with the Dallas Symphony Orchestra, I have come to realize what I was exposed to from such an early age was really a form of communication. I believe in fact, it was an actual language to which I was being exposed. It was the language of emotion generally known as "music."

I enjoy many different genres of music, not just classical music. If a particular type of music communicates a distinct image, mood, or emotion, I enjoy it. As a listener, the more types of music I expose myself to, the more I understand and comprehend this universal language. As a performer, the more proficient I become on my instrument, the more fluent I become in this language called music.

Emotions are very private and personal. This is also the case with music. There is not one genre of music that appeals to everyone. Some like this type and others like that. There is not a right or wrong, or better or worse type of music. Every human being has the ability to see the world as they choose. The human experience supplies an infinite number of feelings and emotions. Whether it is an elegant Brahms Symphony, a twangy Hank Williams Country and Western song, or a mystical Bulgarian folk tune, music is an attempt to communicate these emotions by the composer and performer to the listener.

Music can also be performed in private for personal enjoyment. How many times have you expressed yourself through music when you are alone? Perhaps in the shower, the car, or just walking down the street. We use this language to enhance, express and sometimes even alter our own moods.

There is not a day that has gone by for as long as I can remember when I did not have a song or melody going through my mind. The numerous types of music that I listen to speak to me in a very distinct way. This love of music is something no person can ever take away from me. It is mine alone to shape, cultivate and experience the way I choose. Every day I look forward to listening to some type of music which is interesting and stimulating. I feel extremely fortunate to have a knowledge and understanding of music which allows me, to a certain extent, to control my environment and effect my perception of the world around me. In this respect, perhaps music is the most powerful language of all.

Petronel

"Music takes us out of the actual and whispers to us dim secrets that startle our wonder as to who we are, and for what, whence, and whereto." –Ralph Waldo Emerson.

I've learned that the outcome is seldom a satisfactory aspect in music. It is in the process where we have our best moments and most rewarding experiences.

I've learned that music has opened doors for me and lead me down roads I would never have had the privilege to explore, had I not pursued music.

I've learned that no matter what, the show must go on. I've played during tornado watches, earthquake after shocks, leaking ceilings, with pneumonia, broken shoes, squeaky chairs, unresponsive instruments and noisy audiences. I have also played on some of the world's most amazing instruments and in the most amazing concert halls. Those are the events I remember, the events I hope to repeat. I know every day that my love for music is the reason I am there and will hopefully continue to be there.

I've learned that all the external factors in music, not limited to, but including business politics, jet lag, annoying event planners and bad instruments, are par for the course. We know that at the end of the day, it is the love of music that keeps us all going.

I've learned that when I practice piano, I can work for hours without seeing any real, tangible results. On some days, I bake a cake, simply for the instant satisfaction baking brings to my life. Yet, in spite of the frustration and time, I'm not giving up yet. I know the effort will eventually be rewarded.

Music has been my biggest joy and the biggest frustration in my life. I can't imagine life without it, yet, at times, on a bad day, I might even wish for something to replace that. In spite of this ambiguity, I still wake up every day and go practice.

I'm often reminded that solitary confinement is used as punishment for prisoners, yet I do it to myself, voluntarily, every day. The tremendous joy, satisfaction and reward that comes from my own solitary confinement, I can't express in words.

Edwin and Frances

Because we believe that "all God's critters get a place in the choir," our desires have been to include in our music studios' schedule any person who seeks instruction. This philosophy has allowed us to help very handicapped students (mentally and physically) as well as everyday students and unusually gifted students to be excited with their discipline and ultimate success. Music connects people spiritually, emotionally, intellectually; music can be therapeutic, inspiring; music can encourage civility and can bring inner peace. It is truly an international language that can soothe our souls. –Frances

What a joy and privilege to help someone to learn the piano and organ. –Edwin

Dennis

Composing music for students at all levels has allowed me to "discover myself" in ways I would never have imagined before. It is true that, as a performer, we often "bare our souls" to an audience through our interpretation of the music. But when one is actually writing the music, the level of transparency is even more clearly defined. So often, my whole range of emotions is expressed through the music that pours out of me—sometimes effortlessly, and sometimes with great effort and careful thought.

I've always felt fortunate that I could play the piano— it is truly a most marvelous way to connect with one's innermost thoughts and emotions. When I lost my 23-yr. old son in 1998, music always provided unending comfort when words often failed. Playing a Chopin "Nocturne" or Brahms "Intermezzo" was indeed medicine for the soul. A few months later, I felt compelled to begin composing again and decided to write a collection of music in his memory. I had often read about the concept of "divine inspiration," but had never really experienced it personally until then. All of a sudden, music was pouring out of me almost as if a "higher power" was dictating what to write. It was both startling and exhilarating.

After this collection (entitled *With These Hands*) was completed, I felt so grateful that I had been blessed with wonderful teachers and supportive parents who always encouraged me to study music. For someone who is both a performer and composer, music has indeed been "chicken soup for the soul" and I feel that the quality of my life has been greatly enriched through the music I'm able to compose. In addition, knowing that so many students are motivated and inspired by what I have written is the ultimate "high." Composing and performing music has indeed provided a foundation that supports and enhances so many facets of my life.

Erin

I wake up every day of my life and am thankful for the opportunity of a career in music. I started playing the oboe at age 7, and I knew by seventh grade that I wanted to make music my career. I had wonderful teachers, mentors, and great support from my parents, which all helped tremendously. Having a passion for playing an instrument does not guarantee opportunities or success in the music field. I feel so fortunate to now be the principal oboe with the Dallas Symphony and a professor at Southern Methodist University. I do get paid to be a musician, but that fact is far down on the list of why I do it.

Music to me is an unparalleled form of communication. It can touch the human soul in a way that words usually cannot. It can express love, humor, sadness, hope, strength, peace... the possibilities are endless. To me, each and every performance is an opportunity to change a person's day; to help someone feel a certain emotion; to reach out to a person whom I have never met. It's an art that truly helps to color the world in all sorts of important ways, whether it be part of a celebration, ceremony, or even a movie or television show. My job, then, is to bring music to life for those who need or desire to hear it.

I have a performance ritual that very few people know about. As I'm warming up before a concert and the audience members start to wander in, I look for people who look like they may need the touch of music. It could be a person who looks like they have had a tough day, or a child who is so excited to be in the hall hearing a concert for the first time... the criteria varies as much as the music itself does. In my own mind I then play for that individual in the performance. I can't imagine playing music with a focus on something other than the people I'm playing for, so I try to bridge the orchestra/audience gap and bring them up onstage with me! I love the art of music, playing the oboe, and trying to improve each and every day in this lifelong pursuit. What is most important to me, however, is knowing that I'm making a difference to those who hear me.

Grace

On March 14, 1981, a "China Air" plane landed at the San Francisco International airport. I was a young girl and a passenger on that plane with braids in my hair, carrying two suitcases and $40 in my pocket. When I stepped out into the open air, I couldn't believe that I was actually standing in the land of freedom. I knew my life would change forever from that day.

I was born in Shanghai, China. My father was a pastor, my mother was an English teacher in one of the best high schools in Shanghai. When I was five years old, my parents decided to let me start piano lessons. For the first three years of my piano study, I went to my mom's friend's house to practice after school. I remember vividly that kids in that neighborhood used to mock me. They would throw small rocks at the window where I was practicing. In my young heart, I hoped that some day I could practice in my own home on my own piano. That day finally came when my parents eventually borrowed enough money to buy me a brand new piano! At the end of my 6th grade, I was facing the decision of going to the normal junior high school or the Conservatory preparatory school. What I didn't know was that the world around me was about to change.

Soon, under Chairman Mao's command, the "Cultural Revolution" swept the entire mainland of China. Schools, factories and businesses were closed. The government warned the country to get rid of all Western culture and influences, such as religion, music, and art. Education was banned. Professionals, intellectuals, and artists were punished. I didn't understand what was going on politically, but one thing did affect me. I was not allowed to play the piano any more. It was a crime. Music scores were burned. Many of my parents' belongings were taken away. But to our surprise, my piano remained in our home. Day after day when I walked by it, I hoped someday I could open the lid and play it again.

In order to "brain wash" us, we were forced to go to a farm and be re-educated by peasants. I was placed in a rice farm far away from Shanghai, about sixteen hours by train. There were nine of us there. We lived in an old vacant farmhouse where there was no electricity, no running water, and no toilet. The dirt floor was strange to me, but wasn't too hard to get used to. The wood-burning stove required us to go to the mountains and gather firewood once a month. The light of the oil lamp barely did anything at night. I have seen leeches that were so fat and so full from drinking the blood from my legs that they literally dropped to the ground, leaving my legs bleeding non-stop. What haunted me the most, though, was "Would I ever be able to leave this place? What will I do in the future?" I remember looking down at my yellow, cow-manure stained fingers, wondering if I would ever play the piano again.

Three years passed. I became quite a skilled rice farmer. I had a little, green 48 bass accordion. The people in the village loved my playing. But what they didn't know was that I missed my home and my piano so much that every time I played that accordion, I could not stop my tears. To make a long story short, I was later accepted to be the pianist in a city's newly established Theater Production Company. I left the rice farm because of my piano skills.

The Cultural Revolution officially ended in 1976. Two years later, I was able to attend a local college after it reopened. Finally, we were allowed to play western music again. I remember that my mom used her lunch time to hand copy "Chopin Etudes" on hand drawn staff papers for me. Our overseas friends mailed us books of Bach and Mozart. In the second year, due to a teacher shortage, I was asked to teach the lower classes.

My biggest dream became true when I was accepted to study at Point Loma College (today's Point Loma Nazarene University) in San Diego, California. Not knowing too much English, I left my motherland with hope and love in music. It brought me to Texas, and brought me to you today. Now, my calling is to pass on this legacy to my children and to my students.

Morty

I began piano lessons when I was seven years old. My father was a violinist, my mother a pianist, so it was just assumed that I wanted to play a musical instrument and specifically, the piano. I didn't. But being too young to argue, I dutifully began my lessons. After some years, I became pretty good at it, in fact, very good – or so I thought.

But honestly, it meant nothing to me. I could play fast, I could play loud, I could play almost anything put in front of me. But I had little understanding of what I was doing. That went on until, at the age of 15, my parents changed my piano teacher. My new teacher had a studio very near Carnegie Hall in New York City. I walked into his studio pretty certain I would soon be preparing for my Carnegie debut.

My teacher's name was Henry and the first thing he asked me was to play something. I chose "Rustle of Spring" by Sinding, a Norwegian composer. I never played it faster or louder and I made no mistakes. Surely he had to be impressed with my performance - so I was a little surprised and disappointed when he said nothing. In fact, he looked at me rather oddly. Finally, he spoke. "What was the name of that piece?" he asked. I wondered for a moment why he hadn't remembered. "Rustle of Spring," I said again. "Did that sound like Spring to you?" he asked. "Did your performance have anything to do with Spring?"

"Look," he said, "Central Park is a short walk from where we are now. As this is spring time, I'd like you to walk over to Central Park and observe the trees, the breeze, the flowers, the birds, the people. Let's stop the lesson so you can walk to the Park and observe what spring is really like. You probably never thought about it before. Then I want you to come back next week and play "Rustle of Spring" again, but this time, I want you to think about how best to play this piece to suggest Spring. While you're at it, see if you can find anything about the composer, where Sinding comes from. In other words, I want you to immerse yourself in the project and let your playing reflect everything you know about the piece and the composer. But what I especially want to see and hear is your own feelings included in the performance."

I was shocked. Wow! I guess you would call it my Eureka moment. The next week when I played "Rustle of Spring" again, I got a big smile from Henry when I finished. He told me I played the piece much better and he was more impressed with my abilities this time than he was the previous week. Then he said something I've never forgotten. "Morton, meaning no disrespect, I have a number of students whose technique is far better than yours. While technique is important, it's not everything. What's equally or perhaps more important is what you add to the music. Almost every pianist can play the music as it is written. What makes the difference in performers is what you bring to the music that is your own."

From then on I became much more aware of what was going on around me. When I was learning "Clair de lune" by Debussy, I walked outside in the moonlight and noted what I saw, what I felt. I had never approached music in this way before. It wasn't long after that I became much more observant of nature, people, buildings, stars, in fact, everything. Music, Henry, and my lessons started me down a path that I am still on today – being aware of and appreciating what is going on around me.

I recently read a book review that included this quote, "Music has unique qualities – it goes right to the heart, bypassing the brain. It raises your spirits no matter what your situation is." Would I have ended up differently without those first two lessons with Henry? I'll never know. But because of him, music changed the way I perceived the world, and for that, I will always be grateful.

Stanley

Music is the distillation of human emotions and experiences. It is, for me, the most ideal of all the arts. It's much broader and doesn't have as many confines as other art forms. Like the dramatic arts, music is a play or a story or an emotional situation. You can re-experience life's situations through music.

The first time I heard a piano, at age four, I fell in love with the sound. Before I began lessons, I would sit at the bench and pray, "Please God, let me know how to play the piano!" At this point in my life, I keep playing, because I keep wanting to get it right.

Classical music can be a sublime experience. When you listen to pop or country music, for the most part, it starts and goes until it's over, it doesn't waste time with silences or contrasts. Classical music isn't like that; life is not like that.

People are not aware what goes on inside of me. I experience a wide range of emotions when I play. A musical piece is a drama and that is what I want to get across to the listener, not in words, but in sound. I feel deficient in the way I express things in life. I have always been misinterpreted. What people thought about me is not who I am. I can be much more precise with music. There are some people, over the years, that have shown a special interest in hearing me play and I am so touched by that. That's what you strive for in the music, for the listener to accept your playing no matter how different it may be. When that happens, it is a great compliment.

April

I began learning piano at the age of 32 along with my son who was 9 at the time. Twenty-one years after starting lessons I opened a music school which now has over 400 students of all ages and employs 15 teachers. As I look back over my musical journey, what was a mystery to me before now makes perfect sense—I never realized where it was leading and my husband often asked "Why are you doing this?" As a French teacher at Lamplighter School, I was learning how to teach children in a positive, encouraging atmosphere and learning how the mind and brain of a child develops. Through my study of music I was honing my skills that I now share with my students and fellow teachers at my Conservatory. The mission statement at the Conservatory states that we will teach each student to his or her potential, and from my own experience I know that each of us has a well of unlimited potential if we are fortunate (and maybe stubborn) enough to tap into it.

So, regarding music—first, I was self-taught, then taught by great teachers, and now I teach. I teach to share the beauty, passion, love and excitement I find in music with others, and to inspire them to do their best in music making and in life; to experience the thrill of excellence and accomplishment.

Now music is my life, and by the way, never listen to someone who tells you it's too late!

Richard

Music represents a journey of self-discovery. In all phases of my life, through high school and college, in finding my first job and in settling on a career, music has opened doors, created opportunities and taken me to situations and people that I would otherwise never have had the chance to experience or know. These experiences and relationships have been some of the most cherished in my professional career.

As I have gotten older my perspectives have changed and I have realized that regardless of how important music and the arts are to our world, other disciplines share an equal plane. In other words, I have learned that any endeavor, skill or creation, requires the same dedication and passion as music. Like music, only through constant study, self-improvement and practice can you elevate any discipline to an art form. Furthermore, creativity is not limited to the chosen few who have the artistic temperaments associated with musicians or other artists. Creativity is a way of seeing or sensing possibilities and having the tenacity to make them come to life. When an artist or musician is creative they are said to be "artistic" or "inspiring;" when a mathematician or economist is creative they are said to be "innovative" or "visionary." In the end, they are the same thing.

There was a time when everything I did revolved around music; I lived and breathed music every day. Now, though music remains at the center of my life, it has become a catalyst that has enabled me to explore and find new means of fulfillment. In particular, that evolution has lead me to combine photography, music and writing – things that I have been doing all of my life – into an interactive relationship with each other. Music opened my ears and heart, photography taught me to see and pay attention more acutely and writing taught me to think more clearly and to make music in a different way.

But I have also reaffirmed that only music can move me in ways that nothing else can. It connects me and all of us with the deepest part of ourselves and creates a sub-conscious understanding between people that brings about communication in that proverbial "universal" language where language needs no words.

Felix Mendelssohn once wrote that there is no difference between art and life. I live by those words and I hope that the world will once again place a higher value on art and bring it back from the fringes of our society to the center of our lives. Imagine the possibilities were that to happen…

An Interview With Richard Rejino
By Barbara Kreader

What did music mean to you when you started this project?

Fundamentally, I've known that music has been at the center of my life since I was a young boy and as my life evolved, so has the role music has played in it, especially in my professional career. I can't say, however, that I have given serious thought to articulating what music "means" to me in the same way I asked my subjects to articulate. I suppose this is because I have inherently belonged to music for so long that it is a natural part of my life. It is something with which I wake up and identify myself everyday.

How did the project first form itself in your mind?

Even though I can't pinpoint the day, I clearly remember the moment when the idea first occurred in March of 2008. I had purchased *Class Pictures* by photographer, Dawood Bey. It's a collection of beautiful informal portraits accompanied by short essays written by inner-city high school teens who shared what they wanted most known about themselves. The essays and photos were incredibly powerful and I was particularly struck by the students' optimism and how many of them dreamed of being singers, dancers, and musicians despite having endured some pretty horrific things in their lives. As I neared the end of the book – I read it all in one sitting – it hit me that I could give a voice to music students the same way that Bey did to these inner-city youths. At once, I became excited and sat up in my bed and began to think about the possibilities. The title "What Music Means to Me" was also born that same evening. It was an exciting moment and one that I reflect upon often.

Before you started this project, what did you think the end result would look like and be?

Well, initially, I always intended to emulate the book that inspired the project. But, I also imagined a gallery showing at some point. As a musician, I knew that I would be able to relate to my subjects and I knew the kinds of stories I wanted to draw out of them. It's no secret how music and the arts take a back seat to so many things in life and how funding for them is always the first to be cut. So, it was important to me to give music students a voice and express how music has shaped them. Even though I wasn't entirely sure how it would happen, from the beginning, I wanted to use this project to illustrate the value of music in education and in the quality of our lives, to do my part to become more active as an advocate of music everywhere!

How did you choose your subjects?

Working in music retail, I know many teachers and musicians. So, I began first by approaching teachers I had known for a long time and who I knew would have students that might be interested in participating. I also tried early on to get into a few schools, but I was unable to get permission because of school policies and liability concerns. Ultimately, I ended up getting permission from two schools in Dallas, the Hockaday School, a private school for girls, and the Booker T. Washington High School for the Performing and Visual Arts. Toward the end of the project, I began concentrating on people who were working in music as professionals, teachers, and composers.

What was their general response when you approached them?

Oddly enough, I found that one of the more challenging aspects of the What Music Means to Me Project was articulating what it was about, the purpose, what I was going to do with the images, etc. Sometimes, people understood right away what I was trying to do and other times they stared at me in complete bafflement. I will admit, for all my preparation, I didn't spend enough time thinking about how I would explain the project to people. It became very clear, very quickly, that I would need to work on the presentation. With each subject I was able to recruit, I learned to focus my message more clearly and after I had a few interviews under my belt, I used the images and statements to help me communicate the purpose of the project. Almost every person I asked to participate in the project was very enthusiastic.

As photographer, how did your eye guide the visual element of this project – the settings and the poses?

As much as possible, I wanted to photograph the subjects in their learning environments, their school or their teacher's studio. I also wanted to capture them in a relaxed pose, looking straight into the camera because the image works as a duet with their statement. I want the observer to read what the subject wrote and be able to look into their eyes. It is very interesting to observe the transformation an image takes when you first view it and how it changes after you read the statement. Most people will be drawn to the image first, but it is after you read the statement that the person in the image begins their own conversation with you.

Sometimes, I would make an image of the subject looking away from the camera and I used a few of them in the final collection because I felt they related to the statement in a stronger way.

Did you take the photographs before or after compiling the statements?

It was important to me to have the statements in hand before I photographed each subject. When you talk about what music means to you, it is at once something very personal. I needed the time to read and think about what each person wrote in order to orchestrate how I wanted to photograph them. Almost always, the second or third time I read a statement, images would begin to appear in my mind. This process played an important role in the final product. The one time I photographed a subject first, I regretted it.

Did you ask your subjects to write their essays independently of you or did they emerge from your interviewing them?

All of my subjects began by writing their statements on their own. So many of the statements I received were wonderful and contained compelling stories that needed very few changes. In the editing process, I tried never to change the words a subject wrote unless it was an obvious grammatical error, and even then it was usually only a word or two. For purposes of clarity and brevity, I deleted sentences or paragraphs that I felt were not needed.

Some of the statements I received were what I call pretty generic. For example, they included phrases such as "music makes me relax" or "music helps me get rid of stress," and several other clichés, but not much personal reflection. While I don't deny that music does these things very effectively, it didn't make for the most stirring narrative! For some people, writing about something so personal is an intimidating prospect and not everyone is able to express themselves as well in writing as they are in verbalizing. So, in these cases, I recorded a 20-30 minute interview with the subjects and asked them to expand on their thoughts. They were always able to give me what I wanted at some point. Afterwards, I would meld what they wrote with what they said in the interview for their final statement.

Did any of the musicians discover something new about themselves or their relationship to music during this process?

I really believe that for each one this exercise gave them a new or different perspective. The whole act of writing even one sentence requires you to clarify your thoughts and choose words that describe exactly what you mean. For many of my subjects, this exercise brought a certain validation to their love for music. It helped them to see the value of music, what it means to them and how music influences others around them. The high school students, in particular, were very eager and excited to be a part of the project. At the end of our work together, each of them told me that they really enjoyed the process of writing and being photographed or that they were glad they participated in it.

One of the many patterns that emerged from the statements was that all of them had at least one nugget of gold in it. Every one had a phrase or sentence that was very poignant or revealing. I would look for these inspired phrases to help me get to know the subjects and to begin my own process in photographing them. I was also struck by the depth of what these students had to say. In these last months, I don't remember being so moved – and repeatedly brought to tears – as I have been by the purity of words that music has inspired these people to write. I know that I am very close to this project and I have read these statements so many times that I can recite parts of them, but I have never tired of reading them and when I present them to a group of people, I always feel the emotion well up inside me. To me, this is an indication of the power of the music behind those words.

What experiences stand out?

There are many. Each encounter, each person that I met has a special memory for me. I remember them as if I photographed them yesterday.

I will never forget meeting Riley. As part of recruiting students to participate in the project, I made a brief presentation to her piano class at the Booker T. Washington High School in Dallas. Afterwards, she came to me without introduction and said, "You'll have my statement by the end of the day." I didn't have time to say anything before she turned and walked away. Sure enough, by sixth period, she spotted me in the hallway and with a hint of a smile on her face, she presented me with her statement. I opened the sheet of paper she handed to me and within the first two sentences I knew that I couldn't finish it. Her statement deserved a reading without distractions or interruptions. It turned out to be one of the most moving, heartbreaking, and uplifting stories you will read.

Riley was typical of the students I photographed at the Booker T. Washington High School with her openness and courage. Perhaps this is because Booker T. is a high school for the performing and visual arts and the students there are extraordinarily passionate and articulate in expressing themselves about music. Perhaps it was because these students are so young and full of enthusiasm that their passion poured out onto the page and out of their eyes when they looked into the camera.

The entire experience at Booker T. Washington was extraordinary, to say the least. When you consider that this is a place where the arts are valued in a way that is unique from other more "comprehensive" schools, you begin to see the possibilities of what the world could be if all things were approached as art. In the words of one student, "If the world were like Booker T. Washington, there wouldn't be any wars, we would all get along." There is such an economic and cultural diversity at Booker T., yet the students are there for a common purpose that transcends any differences they might have. I witnessed it on several occasions in the weeks that I was there shooting.

Did any unforeseen experiences during the project guide it in a direction different from your original vision?

Once the project began to get its legs under it, there were several outgrowths from the original idea of the book that evolved. For example, it occurred to me that I might have opportunities to speak about the "What Music Means to Me Project" to teacher organizations and educational groups. So, I began recording my subjects reading their statements aloud. These audio versions have brought their statements to life and they have become even more powerful and more effective. I must say that I feel extremely privileged to present these moving and inspiring stories to teachers and other music related groups because the material speaks for itself and is communicated in an emotionally palpable way. The research supporting the benefits of music study notwithstanding, it is my view that when you understand what music is in a deeper and internal way, you make the connection not just intellectually, but personally. It can serve to convince people more decisively to value music.

Early on, I created a website (whatmusicmeanstome.org) to use as a means for prospective subjects to see what others had written and give them direction in writing their own statements. But as the book and the presentations began to take shape, the function of the website also changed. Now, through my presentations and after an article about the website appeared in *Clavier Companion Magazine*, several teachers have told me that they are requiring their students and prospective students go to the website to inspire them and see the power that music can have in a person's life. Some have even had their own students write about what music means to them!

My hope for the future of the project is to further develop it by continuing to collect more subjects and refine my presentation. I hope to produce a DVD of the project to reach more people and to help open up more speaking engagements. After that, who knows where it will go? I look forward to finding out.

Has this project taken on a life of its own? If so, how?

From the beginning, I have often felt like a writer who, when the flow of words comes from above, is merely a conduit through which the words are recorded. There were periods when I struggled with this project, finding people, coordinating photo sessions, and having to go long periods without progress. I couldn't devote more time to the project because, after all, I do have a full-time job! But with each new subject, it was the project itself, the big picture, that insisted and pulled me to continue and to learn a new level of patience that I wasn't used to! There were so many ideas and possibilities that just appeared to me as a result of this project that I had to write them all down or I was afraid I would forget them.

This project has transformed me personally, which is something that I had not anticipated. With each individual experience there was an unusual level of familiarity and openness. There were times when I was working that I could feel the hair on the back of my neck stand at attention because of the trust and communication I could see through the lens. I have learned that every person has a story to tell, each unique and valuable as any other. If we can learn to ask the right questions and have the discipline to be quiet and listen carefully, we might learn a few things about ourselves in the process.

What does music mean to you now that you have completed the project?

Inevitably, I knew that I would have to write my own essay about what music means to me. My son reminded me of this and, for better or worse, I have included it in this collection. Music is still the only art form that reaches me more deeply than any other. It is, in the words of my former teacher, the most complete of all the arts. Just as every person has a story to tell, every composition is a dramatic story in itself. Some music we use to communicate a part of ourselves, some music we use to help find ourselves, and some music leads us to a greater calling, but always, music is at the center of my life and a filter through which everything must pass.

CONTRIBUTORS

An author and frequent conference speaker, **Brian Chung** is Senior Vice President of Kawai America Corporation, chair of the MTNA Foundation Fund Development Committee and a 2004 MTNA Foundation Fellow.

A selection of his speeches on the subject of music making can be found at www.brianchung.net.

Barbara Kreader is a Keyboard Consultant for Educational Keyboard Publications to the Hal Leonard Corporation in Milwaukee, Wisconsin. A graduate of Northwestern University, Kreader earned a M.M. in piano performance in 1974 studying piano with Laurence Davis and piano pedagogy with Frances Larimer. The editor of Clavier magazine from 1982 – 1988, Kreader has published articles in Clavier, The Piano Quarterly, and Keyboard Companion.

One of the co-authors of the Hal Leonard Student Piano Library, Barbara Kreader has given workshops in over 130 cities in the United States, Canada, Australia, China, Taiwan, and Malaysia.

RICHARD REJINO PHOTOGRAPHY

www.rejinophotography.com
www.whatmusicmeanstome.org

Contact and public speaking information:
richard@rejinophotography.com
Carrollton, Texas